ON THE NEWS

that

SAGITTARIUS A* GROWS HUNGRIER

ESSENTIAL POETS SERIES 317

Canadä

Guernica Editions Inc. acknowledges the support of the Canada Council for the Arts and the Ontario Arts Council. The Ontario Arts Council is an agency of the Government of Ontario.

We acknowledge the financial support of the Government of Canada.

NICOLA VULPE

ON THE NEWS

that

SAGITTARIUS A* GROWS HUNGRIER

GUERNICA
EDITIONS

TORONTO – BUFFALO – LANCASTER (U.K.)

2025

Guernica Founder: Antonio D'Alfonso

Michael Mirolla, editor
Cover and interior design: Errol F. Richardson
Front cover art: *Untitled*, Leonor Vulpe Albari

Guernica Editions Inc.
1241 Marble Rock Rd., Gananoque, (ON), Canada K7G 2V4
2250 Military Road, Tonawanda, N.Y. 14150-6000 U.S.A.
www.guernicaeditions.com

Distributors:
University of Toronto Press Distribution (UTP)
5201 Dufferin Street, Toronto (ON), Canada M3H 5T8
Independent Publishers Group (IPG)
814 N Franklin Street, Chicago, IL 60610, U.S.A.

First edition.
Printed in Canada.

Legal Deposit – Third Quarter
Library of Congress Catalogue Card Number: 2024946489
Library and Archives Canada Cataloguing in Publication
Title: On the news that Sagittarius A* grows hungrier / Nicola Vulpe.
Names: Vulpe, Nicola, 1954- author.
Series: Essential poets ; 317.
Description: Series statement: Essential poets series ; 317
Identifiers: Canadiana 20240457765 | ISBN 9781771839754 (softcover)
Subjects: LCGFT: Poetry.
Classification: LCC PS8593.U55 O5 2025 | DDC C811/.54—dc23

CONTENTS

At the End of the Yard

Because
    after much meandering
    I've determined the world is
    that new bicycle,

    its chrome menace:
    Tour de France,
    Giro d'Italia,
    that hill.

And because
    we laid out the table
    in the garden,
    far too much food, in particular,
    the rabbit and grapefruit.

And because
    down this same street
    we'd once been so hungry.

The wine was all we had left.
Everything had burned, as you know.

But especially because
    the roster pinned to that door
    made no mention
    of fame, defeat.

    The brittle excuses
    we'd claim for our own.

Because that day
    the orange monarchs came back,
    then left.

And the night following,
    when we walked to the strip mall
    green mantids swarmed the shimmering tarmac.

    Through the dripping mist
    the tall lights flickered and hummed.

And because
    in spite of ourselves
    also we foresaw
    our books mouldering.

And in them, written,
    our hunger tomorrow, again,
    fierce.

And everyone had drunk too much.
And everyone began to shout.

And our ears began to bleed, remembering
    the hiss-thump hiss-thump of the cannons.

And even after the peace
    we never quite found silence again.

Nor those hours, somehow no longer.

And because — I insist on this:

That carnivorous thing,
    after so many lives turned,
    leans still

    at the end of the yard,
    against the old shed,

    almost untried.

Such Luck, This Life

> … when at last it came to the soul of Odysseus to choose, he searched until he found lying neglected the uneventful life of an ordinary man, and he took it with joy.
>
> — Plato, *Republic* X 620c

Such luck, this life,
to have slipped through the smoke.

This one, stop the blood. And this one if you can.
The others, beyond saving.

Go into the sea. Go!
Without you they drown.

The law is formal and without pity.
Put the black square on your coiffe and say what you must.

The peril is immediate.
Send them to die, for die they will.

Speak! Speak! On your words
an empire and all her souls.

Such luck!

A couple of stolen soda pops,
schoolyard slaps and punches,
a few library books,
some dubious tax deductions,
the occasional tantrum, plates smashed,
hearts bruised.

My left hand,
up Giuliola's skirt, the flowered one.
At the airport, she was leaving to get married —
What were we thinking?

Such luck, insignificance,
the minutes ticking by, the years.

Letter from the Citizens & Slaves of a Minor Dominion

Don't imagine for a minute, Xerxes,
that war will be avoided.

Enjoy them while you can,
your potted jasmines, your peacock garden.

We lie to ourselves first of all,
and most earnestly.

But the evidence swims
with every crumpled bottle bobbing in the ocean.

The cindered forests, the tar-stuck geese,
our cankered lungs, our graveyards.

The worms are shouting now,
stopping your ears won't silence them.

Hegel and Freud agreed on little,
but this they knew:

Nostalgia is not a legitimate emotion.

Our sons in your zinc mines,
we consider them dead.

Our sons carrying your spears and muskets,
we'll slit their throats.

Our daughters in those dark cities
ringed with yellowed lights and snow.

Our daughters sweating in harbourfront brothels,
we consider them lost.

The bill is longer than Penelope's shroud,
longer even than Hano's circumnavigation.

And the worms are shouting.

Don't dream that because your gifts, Xerxes,
were not returned —

Don't imagine it for a minute.

Though we know who will pay,
though we know.

Short Treatise on the Eternities

You're asking me about Heaven, Hell, the other places?

Well, forget Dante. No imagination required.
Just look down the street, knock on a door,
someone'll answer. And if you're still unconvinced,
ask whoever it is washed up on the beach today.
They'll be mum, of course, they'll turn away.
But insist. Look into their eyes, look at their feet.

And Paradise, that banquet?
Don't you think those wings a trifle awkward?
Just how do we keep the feathers out of the soup?
And all that white linen, brocatelle? And the plumbing?
Don't forget the plumbing. If there's eating, there's the other.

And in any case, we're not talking about drinking
and praising, and whoring likely, in time infinite,
but beyond. Beyond that cloudy, clingy membrane
that bags us, atom, electron, fermion; gnat, sea kelp,
the fridge, that cracked glass, the sad cow lowing, Jupiter,
the stars, yes, and their galaxies, the swallowing holes,
I mean to say, that is us, and all and all, and all.

Beyond, neither clock nor arrow, emptier than death.

Of the Bardo, the beautiful islands, the underpassage,
of the desert and also the river I know nothing.

Which leaves us Purgatory, which,
if you must have comfort, which,
if you can bring yourself to believe
a mountain has purpose
other than itself.

And We Are Weighted

The trouble with dreams, my dear,
is we bring ourselves along.

I, for instance, still inhabit
that October evening in Mardin,
that evening we turned, the multitude of us,
my dreams and I. And from that citadel
on its grey mountain, gazed south. South
across the heat-gilt desert, south to Damascus,
Jerusalem, Mecca and our chaos. Gazed
until at last we reached the green-blue sea.
Ours will be a better place, we promised.

Was it so? Was it so?

Orpheus, did you dream? Or were you
simply prisoner to drunk longing?

And Icarus?
Feather-wrapped and harmless boy,
it was the sun, I know,
that lifted you into its embrace.

Such Dreams

… and those caves, the red hands,
the aurochs and horses, reindeer,
the soot smudges, the lines scraped out.

We were there that day, but also
the coves, those rough beaches where the bright ocean
folds into brown sand.

Time's dull knife.

We were there that day, there was a sign,
an eclipse or comet. A sundog at least.

Mist over the marshes,
the river beyond the grey hills,
their round backs to the ocean.

Time's dull knife.

This pen will not help you,
nor that book, its pointed explications.

Nor that boy, his hands
a thousand times over the bison wall,
that warm stone, where the light never comes.

We dab at watercolours,
somewhere a poem scrap catches a tree branch,
somewhere a jazz singer finishes her set.

Such dreams we had,
such dreams.

A Poem, at Night

for Jila Mossaed

She begins her poem
descending
stairwell
after stairwell,
to the silver water
where every night she swims
again with her mother.

Why is it we read books at night?
Not the ones me must,
the others.

Does the moon, do the stars
have a special power,
their age, their terror?

What is it we fear?
Or are we simply ashamed
of what others might glimpse
when we descend
stairwell
after stairwell
into the silver water?

Of the Thread

My love, nothing stays.

That wall, those stones you pressed against
that first time you pulled me to you.

They're gone, no longer themselves,
since that afternoon, a million years before,
they've been bleeding particles, positrons,
throwing off neutrinos, antineutrinos.

From what point do we measure the fraying thread?

They've moved on, those stones,
raced off with the rest of the planet, our star
clinging
to the end of that long, swirling arm,
our galaxy, bumping across the void.

We do it too, only faster,
so eventually we notice
we've thrown off time, become malleable, cloudy.
We're three thousand parsecs away.
Or 52, I don't know, I've never
been much good at counting.

My love, nothing is still.
From what point do we measure?

Stones bleed,
the world tumbles forward,
time tumbles on,
the stones throw off their particles and bits.

Nothing stays.

The ache becomes habit,
it's a knot, a cyst settled into soggy tissue
of what was, and was not.

Lump just sufficient
to wake you a winter night,
to stare at the streetlight on the ceiling

Trying to recall
the joy of those stones you pressed against
as you fumbled for my mouth.

The Cockroach

Don't ring, don't knock.
I'm not picking up, not answering.

I have, as the French call it,
le cafard, the cockroach.

So for today,
so until further notice
I'm not answering, not picking up.

Le cafard

No, not depression,
nothing so plodding, clinical,
so pharmaceutically manageable.

Not angst,
anchored, organic,
defined.

And no, of course not the blues,
impossibly the blues,
their weight, gravel-voiced,
contagious.

Le cafard

Singular, thin, brick-brownish,
slick as fine machine oil.

The standup, perhaps,
after the room has emptied,
dawn as distant as yesterday.

Le cafard

Gregor Samsa
in the morning noticing
he is again a man.

Though the Churchyard Refuse Her

for —

She stepped smiling into the sky.
But not before unhitching her parachute,
it fluttered an instant, was gone.
Write it down:

She lined up her pills on the counter,
47 exactly, far more than required.
But she chased them with six piña coladas,
umbrellas and everything — just to be sure.
Write it down:

The stool was quite high, and clattered.
But silk, it seems, stretches,
her toes brushed the floor as she turned.
Write it down:

Her jump was precise, the driver had no time to brake.
A quarter million commuters were inconvenienced and annoyed.
But the line remained shut until morning.
Write it down:

It was spring, it was Sunday,
the sky was blue, the river black.
But she was tired, she forgot to press SEND,
her message reached no one.
Write it down:

This, the Place

Between the stars and time, hanging,
beneath the porch where the crickets sing,
above the summer when the fireflies blink,
where night's black arc and the arrow intersect.

This, the place I do not wish to leave.

                                        I was reading a book.
The poet said: Words belong to no one, like smoke.

Have you formulated even one question worth asking?
Or is it still all metaphysics and speculation?
The black arc, the arrow, that ponderous other
that shall forever remain nameless?

                                        The river moves,
and is thus in itself interesting. The lake
closes unto itself, is a world, save that leeching trickle
reaching down, reaching. Reaching across empires, their dust,
to the grey ocean, its hidden mountains
the folding earth beneath.

                                        Fish die. Only
the persistent, the dumb mollusc, stupid
as stones, mud, completes the journey.

This, the place I do not wish to leave.

If we sail outwards, will we truly return?
It is a comfort, I suppose, meaning
there is no end.

I do not believe it.
Not the comfort, not the return.

Fuzzy space, fuzzy time. The rest unnamed.
How then do we construct our reckoning?

Today, seven giraffes fell around a parched well,
their legs, their necks drew a star.

This, their mineral end.

Can you truly wish them to return?

Does the edge fold in? Does it fritter away?
Is the arrow turned? An arc, a screw?
This night, peopled and empty?

It is now we must set out,
when the fireflies shut, and the moth
pauses on a brick.

Which way the moon? She asks.

She quivers,
at this intersect, time and the stars
tumbling. It is now. It is now,
the moon, the sailing, the grey ocean waiting.

This, the place I do not wish to leave.

I was reading a book,
the words, as words should, lifted away,
the pages gleamed anticipation.

Return, return.

This night, without stars. Only the learned
by their lamps, their books, will not notice.

Return, return.

But time, as we know from experiment,
is neither arrow nor arc, much less
a hangman's loop, final.

It is

a balloon untethered, a red insult
hurrying into the wind.

On the Attributes of My Soul

I was naked, about to take a shower.
I saw something fall,
felt it, really, grey and feathery.
It began somewhere around my left ear,
floated down,
neither plummet
nor tumble
nor crash.

But when it reached the tiles
it cracked like a porcelain cup,
splashed its bits across the room.

Ah, I thought, my soul — again!

What have I done?
What have I *not* done — again?

You have turned away from God, was the answer.

But God is everywhere, I said, how can I turn away?
Which direction is, exactly, away?

That is the paradox of belief, I learned.

And I was never turned to God, I added,
how then could I turn away?

And in this grand universe,
and since a soul has neither breadth nor height
nor width nor weight, why then
is my soul so small, insignificant,
this grey mouse, this mole or shrew?

Not even a red beetle, green willow?

Does it matter? was the answer.

Are you so self-important, proud?
The mouse, the mole, the shrew,
are these too not God's creatures?

And the volcano! I cried out,
the moon, the comet, the meteorite,
whose souls are these?
The baobab, giraffe, blue macaw, the jay?

And mine so small, colourless,
not even a tetrahedron, a triangle, a point.
Turned to, away, disobedient,
splashed across the floor, like a cup.

The Seventh State

You asked about the states of matter.

There are six:
	Yesterday, tomorrow.
	Up, down.
	Left, right.

Yesterday reflects tomorrow. Tomorrow cheats.
Up is only so because it isn't down,
which in itself carries yesterday, tomorrow and,
of course, up.
Left simply applies a slight orientation of yesterday reflecting;
right does as well, somewhat more aggressively.

Of these all the world is made,
galaxies smudged across our grand, orbiting lens,
the mud at the rivermouth spawning.

And, of course, the seventh.

The seventh,
which, it is in my interest to affirm, is
the space between heartbeats
where poems
and infidelities
are born.

Of Tuesday

I'm looking for a world in which
bad things don't happen on Tuesday.

It was Tuesday I happened upon my ex.
She was looking prosperous.
Toodle-oo, she cooed,
and headed for the frozen pizzas.

Also, Tuesday was the day she dumped me,
and Tuesday my shrink told me to grow up.
Cut the crap, he said,
nodding to the Kleenex box by my elbow.

Tuesday 1929 — remember that?
Tuesday the Titanic met the iceberg, Riel was hanged.
Kristallnacht, Nagasaki, Chernobyl.

It was a Tuesday the angel came.
Mr Genghis, she said, Why such timid dreams?
The world awaits!

Tuesday also, from Crimea the plague shipped to Genoa,
the crusaders sacked Constantinople,
covid jumped species.

Yes, Tuesday Columbus arrived in America —
an October Tuesday, no less.
Likewise the Mayflower, Cortez.

Said Montezuma to his children,
Of course! It's Tuesday. People know,
bad things happen on Tuesday.

Tuesday, if you remember,
Eve met Mr Snake with his applecart,
and Tuesday the rains began.
Forty days and forty nights, et cetera.

Tuesday the cock crowed thrice.
Not Tuesday, you say?

Well it was. I know this for certain,
or should have been.

I was married a Tuesday.
It was the only day open.
People know.

Well, that's done,
said the Justice to my young bride,
good luck with that one.

Tuesday, let's be honest,
I was born.

Poor child, said the mother.
People know.

September, with Leonor

I heard you're to be married,
that he's a good man, and handsome.

I heard you didn't want a ring,
then settled for a beauty.

There's so much to catch up.

It's three years we sat in the garden,
the crab apples dropping.

The streets were empty, your heart was swollen.
We drank tea with cardamom,
just like in Persia.

There's so much to catch up.
Time calls from its cave.

It's sweltering like July,
but August's been by, October's around the corner.

The tomatoes were failures, not a red one among them.
Your mother's in Paris, her brother is dying.

The card you sent me, the one from Botswana,
I put it in your room, I placed it beside your picture,
the one by the seaside, with cliffs.

There's so much to catch up.

I heard you're to be married,
a good man and handsome.

I'm learning to paint, watercolours mostly.

And time calls from its cave,
and time calls.

Paseo de Las Canteras, April 2022

Tip. Tip. Tip.

In the nether ocean, mountains boil,
glass crustaceans dance,
their long limbs test new stone.

Elsewhere, ignorant armies.

Can man or woman, or angel
or numb statue tell me
I will be blind?

By the paseo, in a narrow café
women laugh, their men bored,
bored as men always,
confronted with the day's windless close.

On the reef the long swell
collapses and sprays, the old sun
turns the leavings turquoise.

Elsewhere, ignorant armies.

I was reading that book.
Words crowded, shouting.

Always, the shouting.

They scurried to the page edges,
set onto my hands, crawled up my arms,
squirming tattoos swarming up
through the throat.

There lies the soul,
though no one admits it.

Ignorant armies,
over dust and tree bones.

Tip. Tip. Tip.

Lightless, the glass animals
sweep the sea.

Can no one promise me
I will be blind?

On the long paseo, the wind,
below, the seawall,
the water swallowing the sand.

There were lovers here once.
We were lovers here once.

Starless.

The yellow city reaches over the ocean,
lights the grey cloud bellies.

The women laugh, their sullen men
suddenly join them.
The children, the children.

The swell breaks, white
across the reef.

Elsewhere, the boiling sea,
glass feathers.

Elsewhere, words crawling,
shouting.

Elsewhere, armies.

Tell me only,
I will be blind.

Tip. Tip. Tip.

In This House, Fate

Fate in this house is not Greek,
it does not return.

It is a fog, a well,
white and silent, hidden,
enormous, where
every thing, made, unmade,
forgotten, unremembered,
where every thing
we did,
and did not do
tumbles.

Careless, We Mislaid Them

Careless, we mislaid them, the ancient gods,
or banished them. Our bright instruments:
syllogism, probability, precise induction,
these we used to rend the fog.

Or they left of their own accord.
Weary of the bickering,
they shrugged and wandered off,
like parents of children
who have never known hunger.

Shamelessly I Clung to You

... but now with the formalities dispensed,
and that I no longer hope for better than a thin smile,
a nod, I can at last turn back to this bright life,
its particular geometry and blur —
the goldenrod bobbing, ravenous bumblebees.

Light is useful not only for nourishment, but also
the measure of time, as too this river, plants — sorrow.
And heartbreak holds no interest unaccompanied
by beauty, tedious as that endless blue against which
clouds billow and puff, and tear themselves apart.

If You're Sorry for Yourself

If you're sorry for yourself, consider the stars,
how long they have been hanging.

There is no wind in space,
not breeze enough to ripple a pond,
nor the smell of anything,
mud where frogs hide, old leaves in the fog,
nor sound, nor light.

Only those stars, and they have been waiting.

And they have been waiting
so long they have forgotten how once
they were born
and wanted something.

The Cruelest Science

Do not tell me how a poem works.
Spare me your taxonomies:
slant rhyme, assonance, echo,
metaphor, simile, etc., etc.

Vivisection is the cruelest science.
The quivering thing always dies.
And we no nearer God
than when we pulled it from its cage.

Hamlet in Genoa

Piazza Raffaele de Ferrari, paper boats in a fountain.

Under the arcades, a Piazzolla tango. The women
in their red heels step,
                                        and twirl,
                                                            and brush their partner's thighs.

Night swallows dusk, the yellow lanterns switch on.

Where are you, dear Prince, that I will not go?
Where is it, this dust that consumes us?

Poem of the Poem

for Patrizia Cavalli

On that we agree, Patrizia,
your poems won't change the world.

But remember this: Beauty and Innocence
pull into themselves the wretched flimflam of time.

So too, like a planet swinging round its long arc,
the poem clears the clanging murk of its lies.

Poetry

If you need to say it,
you're already lying.

But sure —
if it helps push the dark away,
go ahead, tell me.

Tell me you believe
in our words.

Proof

I lay last night, again fretting —
    two o'clock; three o'clock; four o'clock …

And dawn slipped into the trees outside my window,
and I noticed how suddenly I had lighted
upon proof of the non-existence of God.

Proof simple, elegant, terrifying:

You're gone, Dan Miller.
You're gone.

The Eloquent Worms

Yes, I speak with worms. This
lockdown or isolation, quarantine,
whatever you call it,
it's been tedious. And worms, they're
really quite pleasant, unassuming,
uncomplicated, pink and wriggly,
linear in their dirt. I'm not
saying they're shallow or soulless. Quite
the contrary, just
they truly listen and don't
drag into everything old intractables,
don't cloud their earthy ponderings
with might-have-beens-had-we.
They converse, are even occasionally
joyful, though also sometimes they
remember the shovel, and pain.

Spaziani's Theory of Poetry

for Maria Luisa Spaziani

Such a strange trajectory,
stranger still the aspiration,
the shooting star, its death
unseen above the clouds.

The Lost Winter

Why do I still miss you, Kimiko,
so much? We both knew that winter,
those long nights were never ours to keep.
We watched the snow in silence —
What was your husband's name again?
I remember your salt-stained boots
by the door, your perfect nails when you
pulled up the blind. It's morning, you said.
Those perfect nails — and that final card,
postmarked somewhere distant, not home.

Of Inspiration

If light-starved could be gooey ache,
and smell — just slightly — of carrion.

Well, there you have it,
where they come from,
the poems.

Yes

Who was that young man last night?

I'd forgotten him through all the years,
shy, but not afraid to touch a woman.

If she said yes — you did say Yes, Yes! Yes!

You stood smiling by a doorframe,
your belly just beginning to swell.

Was it a one that we lost?

Or the one who grew,
                                        and is gone?

Yes, it was me who left the window open,
the curtains fluttering into the green world beyond.

The Ancestors

When at last the sun set
the light refused to leave.
It stayed on, wheedling the night.

Every midsummer it's the same.
The soup goes cold, flies gather, the fish turns,
some pudding or other quietly bubbles.

They don't eat a thing, nor do they speak.
Though I know what they're thinking,
every one of them, in their rotted out heads.

You're here and I'm not.
You're here and I'm dust.

And the Dream Was Majestic

Between the tree and the city with its automobiles
I dreamt — once, and the dream
was majestic: a great wave crashing into a Cape Breton cliff,
an orchestra, in Vienna of course,
its trembling turning hearts into sponges.

But you know the truth of it.

The sun rises,
            does the other thing.

And a crowded street
is mostly noise.

This Evening

The coffee shops are empty,
there's nowhere to cry.

And this evening that refuses to admit
summer is done.

The wind, yes; the leaves, yes.
Narrow sky; thin, silent moon.

That oh so earnest cricket.

Of the Sparrow

Sparrows too have their sorrow and beauty,
grey little things so easily missed.

In this crowd of peacocks and eagles,
I hope one day a sparrow
will befriend me.

It's Not the Freighted Night

It's not the freighted night I fear.
No! Not this oily dark.

It is the day,
the blue-pink east announcing:
we begin again.

This contest,
you in your bright skin,
I in mine,
ill-fit.

Of a Marriage

In the morning sun, over coffee,
on the road, somewhere,
in the grocery store aisle, in passing,

we've spoken these words
a thousand times,
ten thousand, who knows?

And always we've understood each other —

about as well as a Tibetan
and an Evangelical
negotiating the bardo and original sin.

It's been thirty years, soon forty.
One of us will go,
then the other.

Only these words will remain,
dead weeds turning
on an old pond.

I've Stopped Thinking of Suicide

I've stopped thinking of suicide,
there's no point to it.

A year ago I noticed
a finger beginning to fade.
Then the hand, a few ribs,
the left side of my face.

This morning I stood at the mirror.

So pale I've become,
I could see through myself,
the shower behind me,
the dull tiles, mouldy grout.

So, I've given up dark thoughts,
they're always in a hurry.

And some days I'm not.

My Mother, Asleep

Straight as a stone duchess, or queen
laid out on her sarcophagus lid in some windy cathedral
in Normandy or Navarre,

she folded her hands across what was left of her breasts,
and closed her eyes.

Of November

Before the light goes,
consider — Quickly! The sun's
already under the ocean,
already in another country.

Irretrievable this in between,
this when sleet becomes snow,
when foxes set out

loping across the meadow
into silence.

On the News That Sagittarius A* Grows Hungrier

It was in the second year it reached us.
We live, after all, distantly.

We were unprepared, of course.
No one had troubled to inform us of its trajectory,
or of the simple measures known to defeat it.

At the centre, we learned, Ophiuchus
had grown increasingly voracious.

Unnoticed, we thought
perhaps we'd just manage.
When the serpent consumed its children,
it might also consume itself.

Beyond any charted constellation,
distant from even a junior satrap's court,
in our shivering villages,
perhaps we'd just manage.

I am told the weather at the centre
is pleasant, constant and warm.
They do not know ice.

Here, on still days birds drop from the sky.

When it arrived, we took no notice.
It's not that no one died, people always die.

Children, we all wanted the red chairs,
the red chairs framed in chrome,
the chairs of fame and ambition.

But they were never for us.

We have no great cities from which we'll flee,
tired of the light, tired of the noise,
no long black beaches,
where under parasols silk-wrapped courtiers stroll.

Our streets are usually muddy,
our technology and fashions rudimentary,
as are also our manners and emotions.

We express ourselves stumblingly.
Our languages, after all, are devoid of abstractions.

An idea is equal to a stone,
a legal codicil a post,
an argument a stream bed or a comet trail,
an ejaculation.

And love?
Well love, when we hazard it,
an awkward but permanent exchange of shoes and bedsheets.

We ornament our poems with pseudo-science,
caged quarks and the like spinning or barking.
No one's troubled to complain.

What import, after all,
muddled science in muddled poems
in an insignificant language
in a barren land where locks are unknown,
because there's nothing to steal.

And, anyway, so distant
as to be beyond returning.

All communication with us is into the past.

What microbe or virus could assail such rueful life?

Yes, we wanted the red chairs,
the chairs with chrome frames,
the red chairs of fame and ambition.

All we got was rumours,
from the centre, we surmised,
from those cities we'd seen in pictures,
cities of satin and alabaster and red lacquer.

From the centre, where the serpent
ate and ate and ate and grew hungrier.

Rumours of warehouses, ships of medicines, vaccines
not destined for wind-tortured villages
beyond the lazy reaches even of old light.

And the waiting, the waiting, the horizonless wait.

We send you our condolences for your losses.
We've posted our lists inside
of what here make do for public buildings.

We believe them complete, though approximate,
the last census, school registrations,
birth notices.

If anyone should pass,
and the paper holds,

at least we'll still have our names.

This, We Have Known

This, we have known
since before we were born:
this, your forever war,
we have known since the womb.

A child coughs in the next county;
police vans are dispatched.
And we are defeated.

We object, this is who we are;
jets scream off into the sunrise.
And we are defeated.

The bombs begin again.
We knew this since we were children,
we knew this in the womb.

The earth buckles, our houses crumble;
we shout, we throw stones,
this is who we are.

Great ships plow across the glass sea;
the earth buckles, our houses crumble,
this, your forever war.

We have known since the womb;
we weep and we wail,
we throw stones, molotovs.

And we are torn, and we are broken;
this is who we are,
we bleed and we die.

The police vans return, the jets land;
the great ships rise from beyond the horizon,
and we

are defeated.

Poetry, the Sublime Art

Your poem, sulking, better than a painting.
It doesn't need light, or a frame or wall.
You can fold a poem into your pocket,
it lives there happily, nested in the lint and crumbs.

A poem requires no special materials or tools,
ochre from Kush, Carrara marble, China clay or kiln.
It requires only ink and paper — and not even that.
Burn the paper, the poem remains.

Locked away, a poem gains nothing.
Imprisoned, the poem crowds its darkness,
tightens its syllables, readies to spring.

A poem serves no secondary purpose,
it will never shelter or accommodate or fill,
nor will it suffer remixes or covers
piped into elevators and dentists' offices.

A poem gathers the sky, but gleaming kills no birds,
nor does it pop from its moorings, crash down
onto unsuspecting traders and bankers out for a smoke.

Words don't gain weight over summer,
they don't need to diet or stretch. And they dance,
naked, or in tights and tutu or tuxedo,
to them it's the same, stage or street or bedsit.

A poem is itself only, burrowing
into some Greek-named lump or node at the base of the brain,
there where the mad cells spawn.

Open Mic

The first read something from his phone.
It had come that afternoon, he said.
Something about addiction and memory,
or just addiction, or phones.

The second talked through his two minutes.
Let's get to the flood, I thought. We never did.

The third wept.

The fourth and the fifth, the sixth,
one tall, the other wide, one neither,
lived together, had for years,
between last call and dawn.

We're not vampires, said wide.
Well, I am, said tall,
pulling a laugh from the back of the room.

Seven counted and rhymed,
almost a sonnet, a metronome instead.

Eight also had a phone,
played a tune and repeated,
remarkable! Remarkable! Remarkable!
Remarkable! Remarkable! Remarkable!
Remarkable! Remarkable! Remarkable! Remarkable!

Until she swooned.

This, she gasped after four vodkas and a beer,
is about childbirth.

Nine was from Ireland, and not at all tedious.

Nor was ten, though not from Ireland, and stoned.

As was eleven, who was old, probably,
and brought in a cannabis cloud.

It's for my cancer, he muttered.

Doesn't help, though, he said, and began,
For the daffodils, he read, For the daffodils.

Fuck this! He said.

I'll join you between last call and dawn.
You the vampires, the sleepless,
you with your heads full of words and teeth.

The twelfth brought him some water,
and stroked his thin hand.

And thirteen?

He slipped out the door.
It was night, it was snowing.

So we'll never know what the fourteenth,
the last, had to say, or why.

The Poet As Disappeared

for Joseba Sarrionandia

He escaped in 1985,
and since then his whereabouts
continue unknown.

Do you blame him?
Captivity, as we are all learning,
is never pleasant.

Decidedly less so
when electricity, cables, cigarettes
are involved.

There's a great blank
on a police blotter somewhere,
starting in 1985.

The afternoon he stepped
sideways into that other life,
location elsewhere.

The life from which he sends
every year or so into this life,
postage paid.

In a manila envelope
to his publisher, a pile of poems,
return address unchanged:

The police station from which
he stepped out, uninvited
in 1985.

Book vs. God

Thank you for your book, she wrote —
her name was Samira,
we filled a container; it should arrive in two months.

A boy, a youth, let's call him Hamza,
sits in the library, reading.

In his narrow country, which no one can leave,
in his country, between the wall with its razor wire,
its beach with the patrol boats and machine guns,
he has my minuscule window,
4 inches by 7, approximately,
out —

Out to this postcard country of mine, pretty houses in snow.

But God being God, and spiteful,
Hamza and that book,
that book that travelled two months in a container,
are today wedged under concrete.

As is, coincidentally, Samira,
and 15 or 16 members of her family and in-laws.

If I try to read their names to you,
I'll weep.
And you'll lose patience.

So I'll mention just Hind,
age 22 days.

Already It's September

And already it's September,
and I'm still searching —

This is the year

And I'm still searching for a way to tell you,
for a way to explain.

No more the ducks on the river,
no more the sad bench, the weeds, that tree.

No more the wheezy accordion down the street
arguing with the neighbours and the crickets.

This is the year, I'm trying to tell you,
it's September already, I'm trying to explain —

everybody decided to die.

It's September already, no more summer clouds,
white-puffy, pink-curly, grey bellies growling.

And I'm still searching, and all I find
are holes, punched hither-thither into the sky.

And maybe it's that my finger, that I crushed with all the others
under a hammer.

And maybe it's that the howling, and the howling and howling,
the howling.

And maybe it's just the arid logic of existence —
but those holes, I can't touch them.

Though already it's September,
the nights coming sooner.

I'm So Glad You Left

(November 2023)

Suddenly it's quiet.

This is the only address I have.

I'm sorry we quarreled.
Last night it rained.

I collected water,
I'm so glad you left.

I don't sleep well. My dreams
are as always. Frantic.

You're running, bent low,
something in your arms.

Everywhere concrete,
heaps, dust, caves.

And fire.

They'll come again,
I'm so glad you left.

I paid a trucker 200 dollars.
He promised to mail this.

I'm so glad you left,
I'm sorry we quarreled.

This is the only address I have.

I've Tried So Hard to Surrender

I wanted so much to abandon you,
I've tried so hard to surrender.

What day passes I don't lean into the well?
What blind night?

I let them fall, carefully, methodically,
pebbles, coins, keys,
waterdrops, fistfuls of sand,
feathers turning and turning and turning.

Let me sleep, dear life, and forget you.
Let me slip away without noticing.

But, dear life, you've never been one to forgive.

You'll go on, I know that, without me.
The rend we each leave,
enormous, prickly with splinters,
quickly smooth as a laketop at twilight.

Everyone forgets.
It's not that, dear life.

There's a street somewhere, the lamps are lit,
a word or a whisper, a room,
the vague scent of skin and soap just rinsed.

I Have at Last Made Friends

I have at last made friends with my destiny.
Or so I believe, I can't really know.
This destiny of mine is rather taciturn,
not much given to intimacies, to talking things over.
We're not schoolgirls after all.

No, this destiny of mine, this friend
isn't the sort who'll pop open a second bottle
knowing full well you'll soon be asleep,
and he'll be alone with the streetlight,
alone at the table with your leftovers and memories.

So it's hard to tell, really,
if this relationship with my destiny,
this new friendship, is willed,
or simply an accident.

Like my parents first speaking,
that April afternoon on the boulevard,
because she'd stopped to admire a movie poster,
(Gregory Peck and some beauty she immediately forgot)
and because three days prior,
he'd bought new shoelaces
that kept slipping undone.

The Poem Arrived Before Dawn

My friend Rebecca, she sent me a poem.
It was New Year's, the poem arrived before dawn.

The house around me was silent,
a poem by Nazim Hikmet.
He was on a train, to Berlin,
or maybe elsewhere.
Rain spattered his window.

This poem is like you, wrote Rebecca.

It was New Year's, the first New Year's of our lockdown.
We'd celebrated on our neighbour's driveway.
We'd made mulled wine,
brought personal mugs, masked up,
stood appropriately distanced.

There wasn't much snow — enough,
and leftover Christmas lights still draped about.

It's a good poem.
Hikmet remembers how he loves life,
his train rattling through the rain to Berlin,
or elsewhere.

He died the year following, or the next,
too many cigarettes, too much prison.

I'd spent the night counting.
Had we been 12 on the driveway,
even 13?

This first New Year's of the lockdown,
no vaccinations, the limit was 10, outside, masked,
and we'd been 13.

What if someone took ill?
What if someone spread the contagion?
I'd be so ashamed.
I spent the night counting my failures.

But that's a given,
I am childishly anxious and unforgiving,
and it was New Year's, after all.

The poem arrived before dawn,
Nazim Hikmet on a train to Berlin, or Prague,
remembering how he loved life.

God, I love trains!

That overnighter to Montreal,
my mother slipping the porter a pink two-dollar note.
Take care of him, she said.

Those Yugoslav workers,
ten to a compartment, Paris bound.
They took turns between the corridor and bench,
the smoke pouring out each time the door opened.
Eat, they said to me, drink.

Remember when there were Yugoslavs?
Remember when Berlin, Prague were on the other side?

The Gare d'Austerlitz, the night mist,
those bleary lights, that smell again,
old oil ground under steel.
Remember our sleeper to Bayonne, Saint-Jean-de-Luz.
What new life, we asked, for us at the border?

God I love trains!

I was headed east, like Nazim Hikmet,
where, precisely, I don't recall,
only the sun, stretched like cellophane across the sea.

That girl who boarded at Ventimiglia,
she wore a blue sweater, her hair was cut short.
For two hours we stared each other down.

At Savona, her mother distracted with luggage,
she looks back and smiles,
and steps into the past.

On the President's Eulogy for Charles Aznavour

In France, poets never die.

Oh yes they do, Mr President.
Oh yes they do.

If you like to think so, though,
that's fine by me,
you're Mr President, after all.

But for my part, I can say
I'm not in France. Here
the stratosphere is silver cold
and mares' tails portent something or other
I just can't seem to fix.

And as for these rags,
these rags I've knotted across this page,
they won't add an inch to your year or mine,

even unfurled, snapping windfull,
pulling to beyond the end of the sea.

2008, In Which the Poem Occupies

Why Greek? The poem insists. It's our crisis too.

I apologize, dear reader, this poem,
it continues to ravel, it stumbles, rushes off every which way,
yarn caught in a fan, mad cats.

Is the page too narrow? Too short?
Are the margins wrong, some
childhood trauma unresolved? Spite?

Why the *Greek* crisis? Nags the poem.
It was 2008; 2008 belongs to us all.

It was Wednesday we noticed, if you remember,
how it is we live in a shrieking opera,
Valkyries howl, uncoited lovers wail,
the city burning, greasy smoke settles on the sea.

Wednesday the banks shuttered,
the shop shelves went majestically bare.
Not that it mattered, we were out of work,
our currency not worth its paper.

It was Wednesday also, smirks the poem,
you called in the experts.

Mindful of our straits — and the environment,
they eschewed their usual jets, flew business class,
and billed by the week.

Minor officials, sneers the poem,
middle managers at best. Nobodies!

Liquidate your assets, they say.

Technocrats, hisses the poem,
Schreibtischtäter, desk-murderers!

Again, dear reader, I apologize.
This poem — in fact poems, as you know, dear reader,
are not easily managed.

Liquidate your assets, repeat the experts,
precise, mathematical. And lay out their spreadsheets.

Motherfucking mercenaries! Screams the poem.

You're not helping, I answer.

Forget your dusty empires, they add,
you can't eat monuments, drink winedark sea.
These harpies and lovers, your concertina-swinging monsters,
such vast expenditures of energy and air:

Unsustainable!

Mind your balance of payments, they say.
Here's our bill, please check it carefully,
and fly home.

Whispers the poem:
There's a dandelion in your concrete.

The Unfinished Sandwich

Tomato slice, white baladi cheese, rye,
a bite taken from one end,
crumbs.

An ant trudges her burden across the blue countertop.

Ah, if only you'd listened!
Ah, yes, if only I'd listened.

My friend lived her marriage as a mourning.

So without digressing into whether an unfinished sandwich
    is a sandwich not complete
    or a sandwich uneaten

I'll write a poem for this sandwich,
    this ant and her burden,
    our mottled countertop.

A poem, lightwoven, fanciful, a poem flightyearning —

No! A poem lumpy and dull,
    a poem appropriate to this now,
    appropriate to this silence.

This silence.

April 1986

How could we know?
How could we have known?

We clattered around the outer boulevards,
the six of us, wedged
into your 127, your white Fiat.

Paris, spring.

Rain had washed the dog shit away,
the cobblestones gleamed,
the café chairs were chained.

Not that we cared,
we left the others, we went up to your room.

You made coffee, with cardamom.
In the dregs, you said, the future.

That was the night of Chernobyl,
the night we met.

Now That I've Begun to Understand

We pried the stars from the night.
Our spoons were old, some broke.
We used our nails then, shards,
whatever we could finger.

Already we'd wrapped up the moon,
manoeuvred it into its box.
Imagine the dark! Only
the farthest galaxies still unpacked,
dust blurs, grey motes seeping away.

That was when I began to understand,
about you, and your big house.
It had begun with gifts,
a few bright shells nobody needed anymore.

Now everything's crated and caged,
the sand and the sea, the forest behind,
every feather and fur, blowfish and whale,
the jointed cricket, the red snake,
the viscous mollusc — remember the shells?

The trees are potted, the water
dripped from their leaves sloshes
in the iron barrels we brought.

We've lashed ourselves to the sledges,
no need for whips. Sightless,
we know the long path up your immaculate lawn.
Your topiary, your blind statues have nothing to fear.

There's a fire down below.
That's where we'll go when we're done.
The last of it through your grand doors,
that's where we'll end, sweated, spent,
our lungs full of nettle.

The fire will die. And through the soupy black,
peering at those last, distant smudges receding,
now that I've understood, I'll wonder
when you'll call for them too.

Acknowledgements

I am grateful to the editors and publishers of the magazines and books in which the following poems appeared, some in different renditions:

Carousel: "The Cockroach", "I've Stopped Thinking of Suicide".

The Manhattan Review: "My Mother, Asleep", "Now That I've Begun to Understand", "On the News That Sagittarius A* Grows Hungrier", "Such Dreams".

Montréal Serai: "The Ancestors", "At the End of the Yard", "The Cruelest Science", "Letter from the Citizens & Slaves of a Minor Dominion", "Of Inspiration", "The Seventh State", "2008, In Which the Poem Occupies", "The Unfinished Sandwich".

Stand: "On the President's Eulogy for Charles Aznavour", "Yes".

Special thanks again to the staff at Guernica Editions: publisher Connie Guzzo-McParland, associate publisher Anna van Valkenburg, and, in particular, publisher and editor Michael Mirolla, who so generously took on the task of editing this collection.

I am also immensely grateful to Mark Frutkin, Rebecca Leaver, Richard Owens, and Susan Robertson, who have given so much of their time and themselves to read and listen to this and other poems, offering their thoughtful criticism, wisdom, hospitality, and friendship.

Maha Albari and Leonor Vulpe Albari, my debt to you both for your counsel and encouragement, and for your patience especially, is immeasurable.

Leonor Vulpe Albari, cover art: *Untitled*, 2012 (adapted); first published in *Montréal Serai*, 2022.

About the Author

Nicola Vulpe was born in Montreal. He completed a doctorate in philosophy at the Sorbonne, and taught in Spain before settling in Ottawa. His poems and translations have appeared in journals such as *Alba, The Antigonish Review, Carousel, The Ex-Puritan, The Manhattan Review, Mediterranean Poetry, Montréal Serai, Slush Pile Magazine*, and *Stand Magazine*. He has published a novella, *The Extraordinary Event of Pia H., who turned to admire a chicken on the Plaza Mayor*, as well as four previous collections of poetry, including, with Guernica, *Insult to the Brain* and *Through the Waspmouth I Drew You*, which both received Fred Cogswell Awards for Excellence in Poetry.

Printed by Imprimerie Gauvin
Gatineau, Québec